Library of Congress Cataloging-in-Publication Data
Scholastic Atlas of Space.
p. cm.
Includes index.
1. Astronomy—Charts, diagrams, etc.—Juvenile literature. 2. Astronomy—Juvenile
literature.

QB65.S36 2004
520—dc22   2004052144

ISBN: 0-439-67272-4

10 9 8 7 6 5 4 3 2 1   05 06 07 08 09

Printed in the U.S.A.   56
First printing, February 2005

Scholastic Atlas of Space was created and produced by:

QA International
329, rue de la Commune Ouest, 3e étage
Montréal (Québec) H2Y 2E1 Canada
T 514.499.3000   F 514.499.3010
www.qa-international.com

Editorial Director
Caroline Fortin

Editor-in-Chief
Martine Podesto

Editor
Johanne Champagne

Writer
Donna Vekteris

Graphic Designers
Josée Noiseux
Éric Millette

Layout
Jérôme Lavoie
Jean-François Nault

Art Director
Anouk Noël

Illustrators
Carl Pelletier
Rielle Lévesque
Marc Lalumière
Mamadou Togola
Michel Rouleau
Ara Yazedjian
Jean Yves Ahern
Mélanie Boivin

Research and Photo Acquisition
Nathalie Gignac

Proofreading
Veronica Schami Editorial Services

Astronomer
Robert Lamontagne

JAN   2005

SCHOLASTIC ATLAS OF
SPACE

SCHOLASTIC ✦ REFERENCE

Contents

The universe

From the beginning of time, the universe has been the scene of extraordinary transformations. While the first particles of matter formed and organized themselves into atoms, clouds of gases and dust particles multiplied. Billions of stars were created in the heart of these clouds and assembled into many different galaxies. Today, billions of galaxies surrounded by vast empty spaces form the backdrop of the universe. Among them is a spiral galaxy called the Milky Way, which travels through the cosmos like a wheel of light, carrying the solar system along with it.

The history of the universe

The universe is the ground we walk on, the air we breathe, everything in between, and everything beyond! Since the very beginning, human beings have looked to the skies and wondered where and how the universe began. History is full of stories that try to answer these puzzling questions. In the last century, cosmologists, who are astronomers that specialize in the history of the universe, came up with their own theory to explain how the universe began and how it evolved. They called it the Big Bang theory.

The Big Bang theory

Most astronomers believe that about 15 million years ago the universe was smaller than the head of a pin. All the energy trapped in this tiny point would have been suddenly released during a powerful explosion—the famous Big Bang. An extremely hot bundle of energy would have expanded outward from the explosion at high speed. Small particles of matter would have started to form from this energy. Eventually, these particles of matter would become stars and galaxies, spread around the newly expanding universe. Today, the universe continues to grow outward, similar to the way a balloon inflates.

0 second
An unimaginable amount of energy is released.

0.000001 second
The very first tiny particles of matter, called quarks, begin to form out of the energy coming from the Big Bang. They assemble themselves into protons and neutrons.

300,000 years
Small particles, like neutrons, protons, and electrons, come together to form the first atoms that make up matter. These atoms are hydrogen, one of the chemical elements in water, and helium, the same lightweight gas sometimes used to inflate balloons.

About 15 billion years
The universe appears as we know it today, with its billions of galaxies full of stars.

About 10.5 billion years
In one of the spiral arms of the Milky Way, the Sun appears, followed closely by its own group of planets. Our solar system is born.

1 billion years
Scattered around in space, hydrogen and helium begin to organize themselves into stars. As stars organize, they form galaxies, like the Milky Way.

The future of the universe

The universe is continuing to experience the effects of the gigantic explosion that took place at the beginning of its history. From the first instant, the universe began to expand, and its galaxies continue to spread farther apart from one another. Until recently, some astronomers thought that the universe would some day stop growing and might eventually collapse on itself. According to this theory, called the Big Crunch, the galaxies would crash together and melt into a single point. Astronomers now know that the universe will continue to expand forever.

How the Big Bang got its name

In 1931, a Belgian astronomer named Georges Lemaître was the first to suggest that the universe began instantly in a gigantic explosion. A British physician named Fred Hoyle, who was a strong opponent of the theory, named it the Big Bang as a way of making fun of it. Hoyle was unwilling to consider the new idea. He insisted that the universe had always been here, just the way it is.

The building materials of the universe

When the universe began, there were no stars, no planets, not even the tiniest speck of dust. About a billion years later, stars formed from the gases that made up this relatively young universe. New stars are still constantly being formed while older stars are dying out. All the matter in the universe, including gases and dust particles, is in a constant state of change. Around 400 B.C., people thought that the universe was made of just four basic elements: fire, air, water, and earth. The Greek philosopher Democritus, however, believed that all matter consisted of tiny particles he called atoms. His new ideas were forgotten for centuries until an English chemist named John Dalton came up with the atomic theory in 1803.

Horsehead Nebula

Invisible matter

Besides the ordinary materials that make up galaxies, stars, planets, and everything else around us, there is also another type of material in space that is not composed of neutrons, protons, and electrons. This material is called dark matter. Even though most astronomers today are aware of the existence of this mysterious material, they don't know what it is made of.

THE HEART OF MATTER

According to modern atomic theory, all matter is composed of different chemical elements, and every element is made up of atoms. Each chemical element is unique because it contains one specific kind of atom. Atoms themselves are made up of even smaller parts called subatomic particles. The principal subatomic particles are protons, neutrons, and electrons.

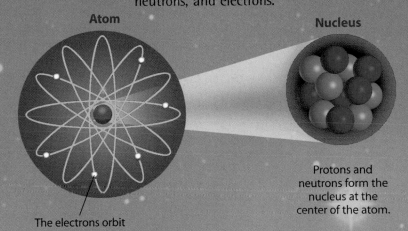

Atom

Nucleus

The electrons orbit the nucleus.

Protons and neutrons form the nucleus at the center of the atom.

Gravity

According to legend, English scientist Isaac Newton developed his theory of gravity while seeing an apple fall from an apple tree. He suddenly understood that the force that pulled the apple down to the ground must be the same force that pulls the Moon toward Earth and holds it in its orbit. As stated in Newton's Law, all objects are attracted to each other. The more massive an object, the greater its force of attraction will be. Gravitational force is responsible for the movements of the planets, the stars, and even the galaxies.

A universe full of galaxies

The galaxies are composed of gases, dust particles, and stars. The smallest galaxies contain millions of stars, while the largest ones hold hundreds of billions. These gigantic areas of cosmic matter are not scattered around the universe; they are grouped together into large arrangements of galaxies, which are called clusters. Scientists estimate there are about 100 billion galaxies that form clusters, which are grouped into superclusters. Even though they are enormous, these superclusters barely fill the universe, and there is plenty of empty space left between them. Using the most powerful telescopes available, astronomers have already observed millions of galaxies. If we wish to enlarge our space map, we will have to explore even further into the cosmos.

Hungry galaxies!

Some giant galaxies are so big that astronomers think they may have "swallowed up" other galaxies that were once in their neighborhood! Even the Milky Way may some day become what scientists call a cannibal galaxy. It is believed that, over time, the Milky Way may "swallow up" Sagittarius, a neighboring small galaxy.

And still more galaxies!

Up until the 20th century, astronomers believed that the universe contained just a single galaxy: the Milky Way. They observed some fuzzy spots in space, which they called nebulas, but otherwise ignored them. In 1924, American astronomer Edwin Hubble observed that these fuzzy spots were, in fact, other galaxies. Hubble's discovery completely changed our understanding of the universe.

Galaxies of different shapes

Galaxies come in many different shapes. Because they are located at unbelievable distances from us, we need powerful telescopes just to spot them. Galaxies are sorted into three main groups: spiral galaxies, elliptical galaxies, and irregular galaxies.

Spiral galaxies

Galaxies that are shaped like spirals contain new and old stars. Spiral galaxies are identified by their curved arms, which form a spiral around their center. Some of the biggest and best known galaxies are spirals, including our own Milky Way, and its neighbor Andromeda.

Elliptical galaxies

Elliptical galaxies are made up of ancient red stars. Some elliptical galaxies are flat like pancakes, while others are round.

Irregular galaxies

Some galaxies have no particular shape. They may look like a twisted saucer or an odd-shaped ball. These are called irregular galaxies.

In the arms of the Milky Way

On a clear night, far from the lights of a city, it is possible to see a large whitish band across the sky. This glowing streak is the light of 200 to 300 billion distant stars that make up our galaxy, the Milky Way. Almost everything we can observe in the sky with the naked eye is part of the Milky Way. Like all galaxies, ours is not alone in its own section of the universe. It is one of a cluster of galaxies called the Local Group, which is part of the even bigger Local Supercluster. The Milky Way is a gigantic spiral galaxy. Even if we were able to travel at the speed of light (186,000 miles per second, or 300,000 km/s), it would take us 100,000 years to travel from one end of it to the other!

Spilt milk!

The Milky Way inspired many myths among our ancestors. To the Vikings, for example, the Milky Way was a bridge for the dead on their passage to heaven. The name "Milky Way" comes to us from the ancient Greeks, who believed that the white streaks in the sky were milk spilt by the demigod Herakles (or Hercules, to the Romans) when he was a baby.

Viewed from above, our galaxy looks like a giant spiral with several enormous arms coiled around a center. The arms are made up of billions of stars of all ages, gas clouds, and dust particles. At the center of our galaxy is an area called the bulge. The central bulge is composed of giant red stars and huge clouds of gases. Seen from the side, the Milky Way looks a little like a sunny-side up, fried egg. The "yolk" is the galaxy's central bulge, and the "white" is the arms. Around the "egg" is the halo, an envelope made of gases and very ancient stars.

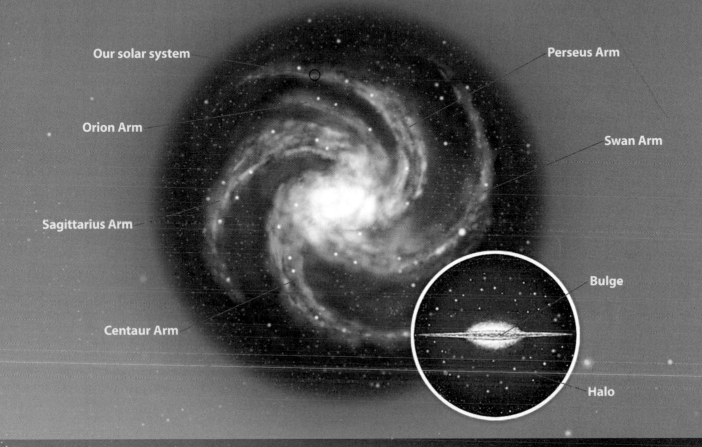

Our solar system

Perseus Arm

Orion Arm

Swan Arm

Sagittarius Arm

Bulge

Centaur Arm

Halo

Our galactic neighbors

The Milky Way is part of the Local Group, a cluster of about 36 galaxies. If we do not count the dwarf galaxies, our closest neighbors are the Large Magellanic Cloud, the Small Magellanic Cloud, and the Andromeda Galaxy. The Local Supercluster includes our own Local Group, as well as several other clusters. The largest of these is the Virgo Cluster, which is made up of about 1 million galaxies.

Celestial objects of light

It was 4.6 billion years ago when a small, yellowish star formed in the spiral arms of the Milky Way and became our Sun. The Sun is just one of the hundreds of billions of stars that shine in the universe. These little points of light are actually gigantic furnaces that produce enormous quantities of light and heat. We now have a fairly good idea of how stars form, live, and die. We know that the smallest of them quietly burn out at the end of their lives, while the most massive ones end in a spectacular explosion.

Just another star

The Sun is a star just like any of the other thousands of bright spots twinkling in the night sky. It appears enormous compared to the other stars only because it is so close to Earth. In fact, the Sun is an ordinary medium-sized, yellow-white star. What makes it unique is that it is our star, the one that gives us light and keeps us warm. Without the Sun's energy, our planet would be nothing more than a lifeless, cold, dark sphere floating in space. Like all stars, the Sun will someday be extinguished, but it's not time to worry yet. It has only reached its midlife point, so our star should continue to light and heat Earth for another 5 billion years or so!

A heavyweight champion

By any measure, the Sun is the most impressive object in our solar system. If the Sun were empty inside, it could hold more than a million planets the size of Earth. The Sun alone accounts for 99.8% of the solar system's total mass. Even giant Jupiter, the largest of the nine planets, appears tiny next to this heavyweight champion!

The solar furnace

Like the other stars, the Sun is an enormous ball of burning, hot gases—mostly hydrogen and helium. At the core of the Sun, where the temperatures are highest, hydrogen atoms experience such enormous pressure and temperature that the atoms stick together and are transformed into helium. Each second, more than 600 million tons of hydrogen are turned into helium this way. This phenomenon, which is called nuclear fusion, releases massive amounts of energy. The energy takes about 1 million years to move from the Sun's core to its surface, where it gives off heat and light!

Even though astronomers have never been able to observe the Sun's interior, they have managed to figure out its structure by studying its surface and the gases surrounding it. We now know that our star is made up of the following layers:

Radiative zone
Energy from the core slowly rises in the radiative zone. It takes the energy about 1 million years to travel out of the radiative zone.

Convection zone
The convection zone carries energy to just beneath the Sun's surface.

Core
Solar energy is produced at the center of the Sun, where temperatures reach 27,000,000°F (or 15,000,000°C). It is in the core that nuclear fusion takes place, releasing enormous amounts of energy that make the Sun shine.

Chromosphere
The chromosphere is a thin layer of gas above the photosphere. Along with the corona, it forms the Sun's atmosphere.

Corona
The corona is a thick layer of gas above the chromosphere. It extends for millions of miles (kilometers) around the Sun. The corona is the outermost layer of our local star. Along with the chromosphere, it is only visible during a total solar eclipse, when the Sun's surface is completely hidden behind the Moon.

Photosphere
The photosphere is the visible surface of the Sun, where the temperature is 10,000°F (5,500°C). This is the part that gives off light. It takes eight minutes for this light to reach Earth.

Solar phenomena

The surface of the Sun is a boiling place, where giant jets of hot gases called solar flares form and then rise thousands of miles (kilometers) into space. When cooling down, the solar flares leave behind darker areas that are called sunspots. There is also a stream of agitated tiny particles of matter that rush away from the Sun at a speed of more than 300 miles per second (500 km/s). This is the solar wind. Once every 11 years, the Sun enters a period of extreme activity, during which the solar wind becomes more intense and the number of sunspots increases. Eventually the solar activity dies down and the surface becomes calmer. Solar activity is responsible for a number of phenomena, including the magnificent colored lights that shimmer in the night skies of polar regions.

Solar storm

Solar activity occasionally becomes so intense that solar wind develops into a storm! The effects of such storms can be felt all over our planet. On March 13, 1989, a gigantic solar storm caused major electrical power failures and many disruptions in radio communications around the world. This solar storm also provided an amazing display of polar lights that could be admired from as far south as Mexico!

Curtains of light

When solar wind particles shoot into space, they hit everything in their path. On the Moon, for instance, the solar wind has reduced some of the rock to a fine dust over time. Fortunately, Earth is well protected from this wind by its atmosphere. On top of its blanket of gases, Earth is also protected by an enormous magnetic field that pushes away most of the dangerous particles. Some of them still manage to slip through, however, attracted by the North and South Poles that act like giant magnets. It is while breaking through the atmosphere of the polar regions that these particles create fantastic light displays called polar lights. They are known as *aurora borealis*, or northern lights in the Northern Hemisphere, and *aurora australis*, or southern lights in the Southern Hemisphere.

NIGHT IN THE MIDDLE OF THE DAY

An eclipse of the Sun occurs when the Moon passes between Earth and the Sun. Viewed from Earth, the Moon is positioned exactly between Earth and the Sun. Blocking the Sun's rays, the Moon plunges parts of Earth into darkness, creating night in the middle of the day! Total eclipses of the Sun are quite rare. Only a few occur each century at a given location.

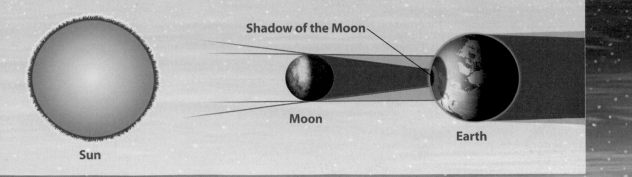

Shadow of the Moon

Sun

Moon

Earth

A star is born

It is said that there are as many stars in the universe as there are grains of sand on all the beaches in the world. In our own galaxy, the Milky Way, there are more than 100 billion stars. About 6,000 can be seen from Earth with the naked eye: 3,000 in the Northern Hemisphere and 3,000 in the Southern Hemisphere. Stars are gigantic balls of burning gases. Like our Sun, they transform the gases that they are made of, producing enormous amounts of energy in the process. Some of this energy spreads out into space in the form of light, which is what makes stars shine. Like human beings, stars are born, grow older, and eventually die. Unlike us, however, they may live for billions of years!

1. The nebula
Inside the nebula, gases and dust particles are drawn together. The center of the nebula becomes extremely hot.

2. The young star
When the temperature at the core of the nebula becomes hot enough, the gases begin to transform. The hydrogen is transformed into helium, and the newborn star begins to shine.

3. The adult star
The star spends most of its life shining while it slowly continues to transform its hydrogen into helium.

The life and death of stars
Stars begin their lives in nebulas, which are immense cosmic clouds of gases and dust. Scientists have nicknamed nebulas "stellar nurseries." The main stages of development of a medium-sized star like the Sun are illustrated here.

7. The black dwarf
The extinguished star is now a dead celestial object called a black dwarf. It is cold and no longer shines.

6. The white dwarf
The core of the old star contracts and collapses on itself. The star becomes a white dwarf, which slowly extinguishes.

We are stardust

When a giant star explodes in a supernova, the material it is made of scatters into space. This material joins the gases and dust particles in a nebula, the same kind of nebula in which our own Sun and the solar system originated. In this way the plants, the animals, the mountains, the air we breathe, even we ourselves along with our material possessions, are made up of tiny particles that were once parts of stars.

5. The planetary nebula
Over time, the red giant's outer layers detach and spread out in space, where they form what is called a planetary nebula

4. The red giant
After billions of years, the star finally runs out of hydrogen at its core and swells 50 to 100 times its original size. It is now called a red giant.

Supernovas and black holes
A massive star ends its life in a spectacular explosion called a supernova. After a supernova, the star collapses on itself. The gases it contains become compacted into such a small space that the star disappears and becomes a black hole. Because black holes contain an enormous quantity of extremely dense matter, they put out an incredible gravitational force. Like gigantic cosmic vacuum cleaners, they attract and "swallow up" any celestial object that comes near. Nothing can escape from a black hole—not gases, not dust, not even light! That's why it is black and invisible!

All kinds of stars

All stars may look the same at first glance, but they actually have different sizes, colors, and brightness. If we were able to travel through space to get closer to some of them, we would find stars that are yellowish like our Sun, as well as red, blue, white, and orange. We would also notice that there are small stars and giant ones, and that some shine brightly while others only give off a faint light. The reason we have trouble telling the stars apart is because they are so far away from Earth that even with the most powerful telescopes, astronomers are unable to examine their surfaces. By studying the light given off by stars, however, they are able to calculate some stars' positions and distances from Earth, the chemicals they are made of, their temperatures, and even the speeds at which they move through space.

THE COLOR OF THE STARS

There are many different ways to classify the stars. One system groups the stars into seven categories according to their color and their temperature. The blue stars are the hottest and the red stars are the coldest.

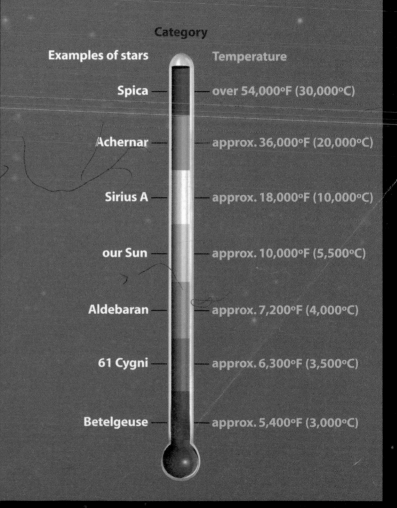

Examples of stars	Category	Temperature
Spica		over 54,000°F (30,000°C)
Achernar		approx. 36,000°F (20,000°C)
Sirius A		approx. 18,000°F (10,000°C)
our Sun		approx. 10,000°F (5,500°C)
Aldebaran		approx. 7,200°F (4,000°C)
61 Cygni		approx. 6,300°F (3,500°C)
Betelgeuse		approx. 5,400°F (3,000°C)

The nearest star

After the Sun, the star Proxima Centauri is closest to Earth. Since it is located 4.2 light-years (about 27,000 billion miles, or 42,000 billion km) away from us, it would take more than 8 million years to reach it, traveling day and night in a spaceship going at a speed of 400 mph (600 km/h). It seems very unlikely that we will travel to the stars anytime soon!

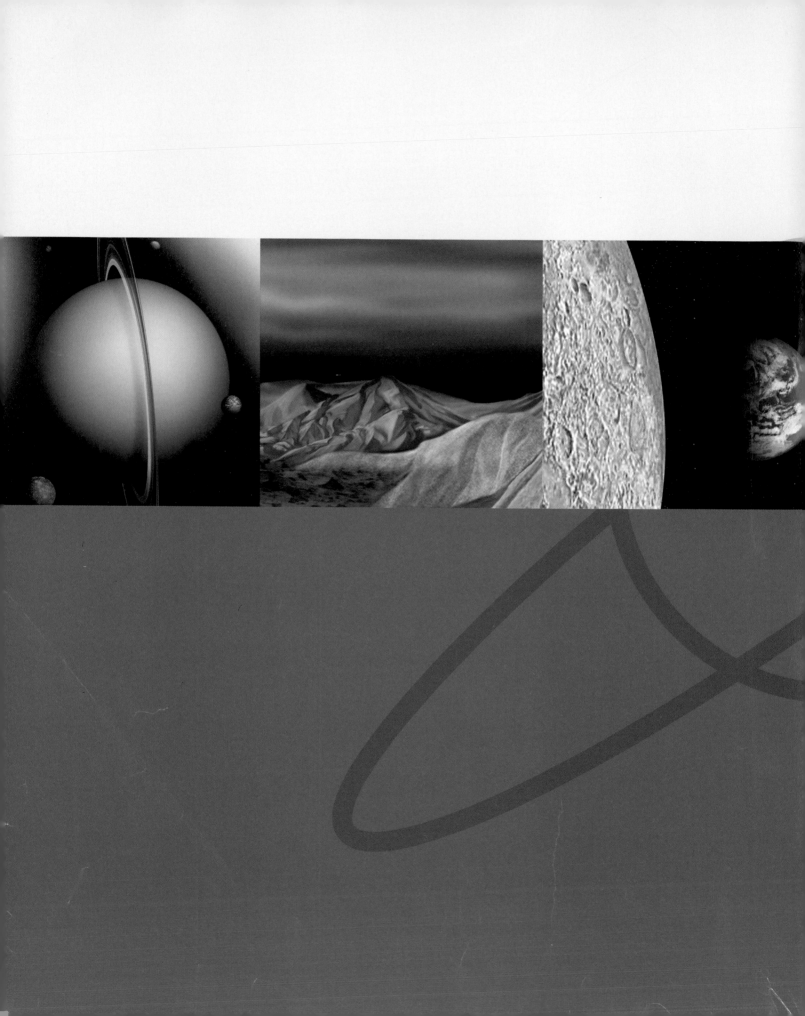

Our little corner of the universe

The Sun is surrounded by a procession of nine fascinating planets. As they move together through the universe, they are kept on course by the Sun's force of attraction. Space probes have sent us amazing images of several moons and planets. As these probes continue their exploration, they help us to learn more about comets, asteroids, and many other celestial objects in the solar system. Even if these objects seem familiar to us, they still hold many secrets just waiting to be revealed.

The solar family

The solar system is our own little corner of the universe. It consists of a star in the center, which is the Sun, and everything that travels around it: nine planets, more than 135 moons, millions of comets, billions of asteroids and pebbles, cosmic dust, and gases. The Sun is the largest object in the solar system. Its enormous mass gives it a force of attraction powerful enough to keep the planets circling around it. It even attracts tiny planet Pluto, located more than 3.7 billion miles (5.9 billion km) away! Each of the nine planets travels around the Sun on its own ellipse, or oval-shaped course. Most of them are not alone on their journeys. They often travel with one or more natural satellites, which are called moons.

THE PLANETS IN MOTION

The planets move through space, circling around the Sun. The time a planet takes to make a complete trip around the Sun is called a revolution. One revolution of a planet corresponds to its year. As each planet travels around the Sun, it is also turning like a top on its axis, which is an imaginary line that crosses it from top to bottom. This movement is called rotation. One complete rotation equals one day on that planet.

Sun · Planet · Rotation · Axis · Revolution

Planets among the stars?

From Earth, five planets can be observed with the naked eye: Mercury, Venus, Mars, Jupiter, and Saturn. At first sight they look like any of the stars surrounding them. Early astronomers noticed, however, that certain bright points of light changed their positions in the sky, from month to month, unlike the other stars that seemed to remain fixed in place. They called these moving stars "planets," which comes from the Greek word *planêtês*, meaning "wanderer."

The planets

The planets are sorted into two different groups, according to what they are made of: rocky planets and gaseous planets. The rocky planets include Mercury, Venus, Earth, and Mars. They have solid surfaces made up of rock, and tend to be smaller than the gaseous planets. The rocky planets are the closest to the Sun. They are also classified as terrestrial planets. The gaseous planets are giant balls of gases. They include Jupiter, Saturn, Uranus, and Neptune. They are also classified as Jovian planets. Distant planet Pluto is in a category all its own, because it is made of ice as well as rock. Along with the Jovian planets, it is separated from the terrestrial planets by the Main asteroid belt.

See activity p. 74

The Sun's little neighbor

The planet Mercury is the Sun's closest neighbor. It is so close, in fact, that it only takes the planet 88 days to complete its journey around the Sun. Observing little Mercury speeding across the sky inspired the ancient Romans to name this planet after their quick-footed messenger god. Although Mercury travels around the Sun quickly, it spins on its own axis very slowly. One day there is equivalent to almost six months on Earth! After Pluto, Mercury is the second smallest planet in the solar system. Similar to our Moon both in size and appearance, Mercury has no atmosphere and has a dusty surface dotted with thousands of craters. The largest crater, called the Caloris basin, measures more than 800 miles (1,300 km) across, which is about half the width of the United States!

Photographs of Mercury
The space probe Mariner 10 is the only one to have visited Mercury so far. In March 1974, Mariner 10 flew less than 440 miles (700 km) above the surface and took thousands of pictures of one side of the planet. Another probe, the Messenger Mercury Orbiter, is scheduled to photograph the other side of the planet in 2007–2008.

Observing Mercury

Of the five planets visible from Earth, Mercury is the most difficult planet to spot, even with the help of a powerful telescope. Because Mercury is so close to the Sun, it seems to disappear from the sky almost at the same time as the Sun, and cannot be seen at night. The only time to catch a glimpse of this little planet is at sunset or at dawn, when it is close to the horizon.

The biggest difference in temperature

Mercury has no atmosphere to shield it from the Sun's burning, hot rays. Without this protective layer of gases, Mercury is also unable to keep any of the Sun's heat on its surface once night falls. While daytime temperatures climb to about 800°F (425°C), a long night on this planet may be as low as -300°F (-185°C)! The biggest temperature changes in the solar system occur on Mercury.

Earth's neighbor

After the Moon, Venus is the brightest celestial object in the night sky. Early astronomers mistook it for a twinkling star. They called it the "morning star," "evening star," or "shepherd's star," depending on which time of day it became visible in the sky. This bright planet is the first to appear when the Sun goes down and the last to disappear when the Sun rises. Earth's neighbor Venus is the second planet from the Sun. It was once thought of as Earth's twin. Venus and Earth are just about the same size and both have a rocky surface and cloudy atmosphere—but the comparisons end there. Venus's environment is very unfriendly, with its extreme heat, crushing pressure, unbreathable air, and clouds that contain drops of acid. In fact, the first space probes to visit the planet melted as soon as they came into contact with it!

Photographs of Venus

Up to now, about 20 space probes have approached Venus. The first ones to orbit this planet were unable to photograph its surface because it is constantly hidden behind thick clouds. It was only in 1994 that the American space probe Magellan managed to reveal Venus's landscape with great details. Equipped with powerful radar able to break through the planet's thick atmosphere, Magellan swept Venus's surface with radar waves. By measuring the time it took for these waves to return to the probe, astronomers were able to determine the planet's surface features. Their computer-generated pictures show large flat areas as well as gigantic volcanoes. The tallest, at 5 miles (8 km) high, is Maat Mons, slightly smaller than Earth's Mount Everest (5.5 miles, or 8.8 km, high). Some scientists believe it might be an active volcano.

Venus is surrounded by several layers of clouds almost 57 miles (90 km) deep. This envelope of clouds acts like a mirror, reflecting most of the Sun's rays back into space. This is the reason that Venus appears to be so bright. Despite its thick cloud layer, some of the Sun's heat manages to get through to the surface, where it is trapped. The heat makes the temperature rise like it does in a greenhouse. It is because of this "greenhouse effect" that Venus, at almost 900°F (480°C), is the hottest planet in the solar system.

The cloud layer reflects most of the Sun's rays.

Some of the Sun's rays pass through the clouds and heat up the planet's surface.

The envelope of gas traps heat and prevents it from escaping into space.

A day that is longer than a year!

It takes Venus 225 Earth days to complete a full trip around the Sun. This is a year on Venus. Venus also spins, taking 243 Earth days to make a full rotation. This represents a day on Venus. Therefore, a day on Venus is actually longer than a year on Venus!

The exceptional blue planet

Like Mercury, Venus, and Mars, Earth is a rocky planet. It is, however, larger and much more active than its neighbors. Along with one of Jupiter's natural satellites Io, it is one of the only places in the solar system confirmed to have active volcanoes. Earth is actually unique for many other reasons: It is the only planet with plenty of water, an oxygen-rich atmosphere to protect it, and an ability to support life. It is also the only planet that has not been named after a Greek or Roman god. The name "Earth" simply comes from *era*, the Greek word for earth. Our planet might just as easily have been called "Ocean," however, because the seas and oceans cover more than two-thirds of its surface. The blue planet travels around the Sun accompanied by a large natural satellite, our Moon.

This view of Earth is from the rear porthole of the space shuttle. Our planet looks like a marble with swirling colors floating in the blackness of space. The blue areas that seem to dominate are vast oceans, the white areas are clouds, and the brown and green areas are continents.

A changing landscape
When Earth was formed 4.6 billion years ago, it was a huge ball of melted rock. As the young planet slowly cooled, the crust began to change into a solid. Not long afterward, meteorites, which are blocks of rocks and metals that fall from space, hit the newly formed crust, scarring it with craters. Over thousands of years, winds and rains managed to erase most of these scars. Through this same process, called erosion, rivers dug valleys and ocean waves carved out the shoreline. Today, erosion continues to wear down Earth's rocky surface, gradually reshaping our planet's features. Earth's appearance can also be changed much more quickly, by earthquakes and volcanoes.

Earth is mainly made of iron, oxygen, and silica, a substance found in sand. These different materials are not distributed evenly throughout the planet. By studying the way seismic waves (tremors from earthquakes) travel through the ground, scientists have determined that our planet is made up of several main layers.

The inner core

At the center of Earth is a solid inner core, which consists mostly of iron. The core is almost as hot as the surface of the Sun.

The outer core

The outer core is not quite as hot as the inner core. It is mostly made up of melted iron and nickel. As these liquid metals move around, they produce a powerful magnetic field that can be detected with a compass.

The mantle

Surrounding the inner and outer core is the mantle, which is made of mainly melted rock. Movements inside the mantle conduct heat from the core to the planet's surface.

Earth's crust

Earth's crust is a thin, solid layer of rock and minerals that also makes up our continents as well as the ocean floor. Like a puzzle, Earth's crust is composed of a dozen giant plates, called tectonic plates, which float on top of the mantle. Moved by the heat coming out of the mantle, the plates are constantly shifting around, much like a lid on a pot of boiling water, slowly dragging the oceans and the continents along with them. Volcanoes and earthquakes occur at the edges of these plates.

Round or flattened?

The Greek philosopher Aristotle proved more than 2,300 years ago that Earth was round. One of the ways he demonstrated this was by pointing out how Earth's shadow was always perfectly circular during a lunar eclipse. We now understand that the planet is not perfectly round, but rather slightly flattened at the poles. Scientists call this particular shape a geoid.

Earth in motion

Like a giant spaceship carrying people, animals, plants, and millions of tiny living organisms, Earth hurtles through space at a speed of more than 60,000 miles per hour (100,000 km/h). Fortunately, we don't feel it because everything on the planet is moving at the same speed—the ground we walk on, the houses we live in, and every object around us. Earth makes a complete trip, or revolution, around the Sun in 365 $\frac{1}{4}$ days. It is during this yearlong orbit that Earth's four seasons occur, one after the other. Like the other planets in the solar system, ours also spins, or rotates. One complete rotation takes 24 hours, the length of time of one day and night.

Day and night

Every day we watch the Sun "rise" in the east, move across the sky, and "set" in the west. In fact, the Sun is not moving at all; it is Earth that is moving. Earth makes a complete rotation in a 24-hour period that includes a day and a night. Because Earth rotates while it travels around the Sun, every part of the planet gets its share of daylight and darkness. It is daytime on the side of Earth that is facing the Sun, and nighttime on the opposite side.

The days are getting longer

Scientists have calculated that Earth's rotation is slowing down by one second every 50,000 years. At this rate, in 5 billion years an Earth day will last 48 hours instead of 24 hours. It will be twice as long!

THE CYCLE OF THE SEASONS

Seasons are caused by the changing amounts of solar energy that strike a part of Earth at different times of the year. Since Earth is slightly tilted to one side as it travels around the Sun, some areas of the planet receive more energy in the form of light and heat than others. Because the Sun's rays strike Earth's equator almost always directly, this area is the hottest. As we get farther away from the equator, the Sun's rays hit the ground less directly, at a more slanted angle. These areas experience colder temperatures. When the North Pole is tilted toward the Sun, it is summer in the north half, the Northern Hemisphere, and winter in the south half, the Southern Hemisphere. The opposite occurs when the South Pole is tilted toward the Sun.

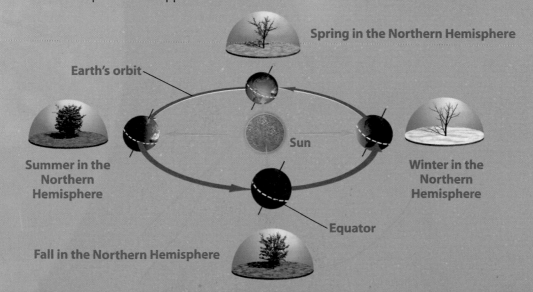

Spring in the Northern Hemisphere

Earth's orbit

Sun

Summer in the Northern Hemisphere

Winter in the Northern Hemisphere

Equator

Fall in the Northern Hemisphere

The fascinating red planet

Seen from Earth, Mars looks like a reddish star. It is nicknamed the "red planet." The ancient Romans named the planet after their god of war. Even though it is only half the size of Earth, it is the planet that most resembles our own. Like Earth days, days on Mars are 24 hours long. It also has an atmosphere, four seasons, and ice caps at its poles. The red planet, however, is not a very friendly place to visit. Its surface is frequently swept by massive dust storms, and in winter, temperatures can drop to as low as -338°F (-170°C). Although conditions on Mars are not favorable for supporting life as we know it, many scientists believe that they once were. When traveling around the Sun, the red planet is joined by its two small moons, Phobos and tiny Deimos.

A dizzying landscape

Land features on Mars are extremely varied. Its surface is marked by immense canyons and huge extinct volcanoes. The red planet is actually home to the largest volcano in the solar system. Olympus Mons, almost 16 miles (26 km) high, is three times as tall as Mount Everest, the highest mountain on Earth. Mars also has the largest canyons in the solar system. Valles Marineris, which is easily visible from space, is 10 times as long as the Grand Canyon in Arizona.

Exploring Mars

Besides Venus, no other planet has been explored as much as Mars. In 1997, Sojourner, a small robot vehicle belonging to the Pathfinder probe, spent three months analyzing the composition of the soil on Mars. It found that certain rocks lay in formations that resembled sedimentary rocks, a kind of rock found on Earth that is formed by water. It also found that there was no life on the planet. In 2004, two new space probes—Spirit and Opportunity—examined the soil underneath the surface. They found additional proof that water was abundant for a long period of time on this planet, but still no traces of life. There are hopes of sending astronauts to the planet around the year 2030.

A planet turned to rust

Mars is a rusty planet! The water that existed on the planet long ago turned the iron in the rock into rust. It is this rust that gives the red planet its striking color. During Mars's frequent storms, huge clouds of red dust particles are blown around, giving the sky its unique pinkish tint.

King of the giants

Of the four gaseous planets in the solar system, Jupiter is the largest; it takes up the same amount of space as 1,400 planets the size of Earth! It has more natural satellites circling it than any other planet. There are at least 63 moons orbiting it. This giant planet almost looks like a sun sitting in the center of its very own solar system. Even though most illustrations of the solar system make it appear close to Mars, Jupiter is actually very far away. In fact, the distance between these two planets is twice as great as the distance from Mars to the Sun. Pioneer 10, the first space probe to visit Jupiter, took more than a year and a half to reach its destination!

The Great Red Spot

Jupiter's atmosphere is constantly being battered by more than a thousand cloud storms. Each one can be compared to a hurricane on Earth. The largest and most famous of these storms is the Great Red Spot, which is clearly visible in all the photos taken of Jupiter. This storm has been raging for more than 300 years, and spreads out over an area of about 25,000 miles (40,000 km)—three times the size of Earth!

It could have been a star!

Jupiter is mainly composed of the same gases that make up our star, the Sun. If the planet had contained just 80 times more gas, nuclear fusion, which is what causes stars to shine, could have taken place at its heart. If this had occurred, Jupiter would have been a star instead of a planet!

Jupiter's satellites

Jupiter's four largest natural satellites were discovered by Italian astronomer Galileo Galilei in 1610, shortly after the telescope was invented. These four moons are called Galilean satellites in his honor. Their sizes are similar to smaller planets like Mercury and Pluto. Since Galileo's time, another 59 moons as well as three thin rings composed of dust particles have been discovered.

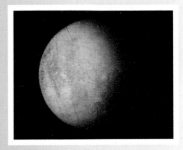

Io

Io is the Galilean satellite that is closest to Jupiter. This moon is easy to recognize by its volcanoes, which are 100 times more active than volcanoes on Earth. Io's volcanoes spray jets of gas more than 160 miles (250 km) high. The gas is composed of sulfur, a yellowish substance that gives Io its color.

Europa

Europa's surface is covered by a thin blanket of cracked ice. It is possible that an ocean of liquid water is hidden beneath the ice. Some astronomers believe that a form of primitive life such as bacteria may exist there.

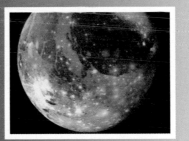

Ganymede

Ganymede is the largest of Jupiter's moons and is also the largest natural satellite in our solar system; it is about the same size as the planet Mercury. Ganymede's surface is covered in ice and dotted with craters.

Callisto

Callisto's surface is covered with craters. A saltwater ocean may be hidden under its frozen surface.

Jupiter's clouds

Jupiter's gaseous surface is hidden under many layers of clouds. Despite the planet's enormous size, it spins at almost 28,000 miles per hour (45,000 km/h). It makes a full rotation in less than 10 hours. This rapid spinning forces Jupiter's clouds to form bands that encircle the planet. Within each band are powerful winds pushing in opposite directions. They are particularly fierce, blowing at speeds of more than 400 miles per hour (650 km/h). The colors of the cloud bands vary according to the type of gases they contain.

The magnificent ringed planet

Saturn is the second largest gaseous planet. It is famous for its beautiful rings, the brightest in our solar system. Beneath its rings, it very much resembles Jupiter. Like its giant neighbor, Saturn has an unstable atmosphere and clouds that encircle it in horizontal bands. The winds in these cloud bands blow at more than 1,000 miles per hour (1,600 km/h)—three times as fast as the winds on Jupiter! Saturn gets its dark yellow color from the fog of ammonia gas hanging over its clouds. Like the other gaseous planets, Saturn travels around the Sun with numerous natural satellites.

Saturn's satellites

Saturn has 31 natural satellites that we know of. Some are several thousand miles (kilometers) in diameter, while others are less than 12 miles (20 km) wide. Titan is the largest of Saturn's moons. It is actually the second largest natural satellite in the solar system after Ganymede, one of Jupiter's moons. The second largest is Iapetus.

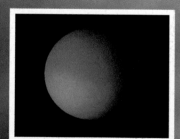

Titan

Titan is the only satellite in the solar system with a dense atmosphere, similar to that of a young Earth. A thick layer of orange clouds prevents us from being able to clearly see its surface.

Iapetus

Iapetus presents a surface of contrasts: The light part is made of ice, while the dark is made of an unknown material.

Saturn's rings

Three of Saturn's rings are visible from Earth. In addition, space probes that have approached the planet have discovered four others. Thanks to American space probes Voyager 1 and 2, we know now that each of the seven main rings is actually composed of thousands of tiny rings. These ringlets are in turn made up of billions of bits of ice and rocks of different sizes. Some astronomers believe that these bits are the remains of exploded satellites or comets that have been captured by the planet's force of attraction. The famous rings cover a distance of more than 186,000 miles (300,000 km). This is only a little less than the distance separating Earth from the Moon!

The planet that floats

Saturn has a low density, which means it contains very little matter despite its large size. Even though it contains iron and rock at its center, the planet is mainly composed of light gases. Saturn is the least dense of all the planets. It is actually so light that it could float on water—if you could find an ocean big enough to hold it!

The planet that lies on its side

Uranus is the only planet that travels in space by rolling like a ball instead of spinning on its axis like a top. Astronomers believe that long ago, Uranus was knocked on its side by a collision with another celestial object. Some even think that Uranus's rings and its natural satellites were formed out of the debris left over from this collision. In fact, we know very little about this distant gaseous planet. Uranus has been visited only once, by Voyager 2 in 1986. The space probe measured an icy temperature of −346°F (−210°C) above the planet's clouds! It also found traces of methane gas in Uranus's atmosphere. Methane gives the planet its blue-green color.

Uranus's satellites
So far, at least 27 moons have been discovered circling around Uranus. Most of these natural satellites take their name from William Shakespeare's plays. For example, the moons called Sycorax and Saliba, which were discovered in 1997, are named after characters in the play *The Tempest*. All of Uranus's satellites are made from a mixture of rocks and ice. Miranda, pictured to the left, stands apart from the others because of its unusual surface. Some astronomers believe that this satellite was gradually formed from bits and pieces that glued themselves together after a collision with a meteorite or a huge asteroid.

A seventh planet

In 1781, a German musician named William Herschel was the first to spot the planet Uranus using a telescope he had built himself. The amateur astronomer's discovery was very important because up until that time it was believed that Saturn was the most distant planet in the universe. Thanks to Herschel's observations, the solar system not only expanded to include seven planets, but it became twice as large as was previously thought.

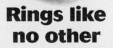

Rings like no other

Uranus's 11 rings may not be bright and colorful like those of Saturn, but they are still unique. Uranus is the only planet whose rings encircle it vertically, or straight up and down, because the planet is lying on its side. The rocks and dust particles that make up these rings are blacker than coal, making them the darkest objects in the entire solar system.

The last of the gaseous giants

Neptune is a frozen world we know little about. The American space probe Voyager 2 visited this most distant of the gaseous planets in 1989. It found an enormous blue sphere encircled by four dark, narrow rings. Neptune is similar to Uranus in size, composition, atmosphere, and color. Neptune's atmosphere, however, shows much more activity than its neighbor. Bands of moving clouds have been observed, as well as an enormous hurricane that resembles Jupiter's Great Red Spot. Neptune's Great Dark Spot, as this storm is called, is about the size of Earth. Here, winds reach speeds of 1,200 miles per hour (2,000 km/h)—the most powerful winds in the solar system.

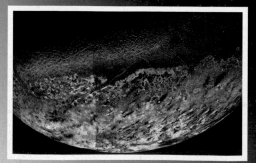

Neptune's satellites
Thirteen moons are known to travel with Neptune in its orbit around the Sun. The largest of these is Triton. Triton is the coldest place in the solar system, with a temperature of only -391°F (-235°C). On Triton's icy, cracked surface, which resembles the skin of a cantaloupe, Voyager 2 found geysers shooting nitrogen snow, a frozen gas, more than 5 miles (8 km) into the atmosphere.

The discovery of Neptune

Thanks to the work of two mathematicians, German astronomer Johann Galle (on the left) was able to see the planet Neptune in 1846. In the early 1800s, astronomers had noticed irregularities in Uranus's orbit. Mathematicians John Couch Adams of England and Urbain Le Verrier of France came up with a theory. They believed that perhaps the force of attraction, or gravitational pull, of some unseen planet was causing Uranus to go off its regular path. By studying this oddity in Uranus's orbit, they were able to calculate the position of the unknown celestial object, which turned out to be Neptune. In this way they located the new planet without ever seeing it.

Sometimes the farthest

Neptune is the second most distant planet in the solar system, except when it's not! This is because Pluto, the farthest planet, sometimes crosses into Neptune's orbit during its 248-year orbit around the Sun. When this occurs, Neptune spends the next 20 years being the planet farthest from the Sun. The last time this happened was during the years 1979 to 1999.

A small, distant planet

The last planet in our solar system is also the smallest. Pluto is even tinier than our Moon. Because it is so far away, it is the planet we know the least about. No space probe has observed Pluto yet, although the American probe New Horizons is scheduled to visit Pluto in July 2015. Pluto is so far away that, in its dark skies, the Sun appears only slightly brighter than any of the other stars. Even the most powerful telescope, the Hubble Space Telescope, has only been able to detect a thin atmosphere and some bright areas on the planet's surface. These bright spots probably consist of a thin blanket of frozen gas called methane. Although Pluto has not been examined up close, there is little doubt that this faraway planet is a dark and frozen world.

Is it truly a planet?
Farther out in space beyond Pluto is the Kuiper belt, an area filled with frozen pieces of rock and ice. To some astronomers, Pluto is merely the largest object in this belt. Not only is Pluto much smaller than the other eight planets, its composition is also different. Like Triton, Neptune's largest moon, Pluto is made up of 80 percent rock and 20 percent ice. For this reason, some scientists believe that Pluto was once a satellite of Neptune. Despite these unanswered questions, in 1999 the International Astronomical Union declared that Pluto deserved its status as a full-fledged planet.

The discovery of Pluto

The ninth planet in the solar system was discovered in 1930 by Clyde Tombaugh, a 24-year-old American astronomer. Tombaugh was trying to find the celestial body responsible for disrupting Neptune's orbit. Instead, he accidentally discovered a tiny planet, later named Pluto. Since Pluto was far too small to affect the orbit of a large planet like Neptune, Tombaugh spent many years searching for another celestial body without success. Since then, the irregularities in Neptune's orbit have disappeared entirely and many astronomers think that the original measurements were faulty. Today, most scientists believe that a tenth planet simply does not exist.

Pluto has a tiny moon called Charon. Compared to Pluto, however, Charon is huge. And since the two astral bodies are so close together, some astronomers refer to the pair as a double planet.

In Pluto's honor!

Mickey Mouse's trusty companion, a dog named Pluto, first appeared on movie screens in 1930. American filmmaker Walt Disney named the dog after the planet Pluto, which had been discovered in February of the same year.

Our own natural satellite

The Moon is Earth's only natural satellite. Our planet's trusty companion is an airless, silent world without any signs of life. Because of its small size, the Moon's force of attraction is too weak to hold the gases it would need to form an atmosphere. Without a layer of air, the Moon cannot trap the Sun's heat to warm it at night or protect itself from too much heat during the day. This makes the Moon's nights freezing cold and its days hotter than boiling water. The lunar landscape has not changed much in thousands of years. The many craters that dot its surface are scars from meteorites that hit the Moon early in its history. The Moon's vast plains are large craters filled with lava, which came out of cracks in its crust. Around these plains are hills and mountain ranges.

WHERE DOES THE MOON COME FROM?

By analyzing the lunar rock samples brought back by astronauts, scientists have been able to piece together the Moon's history. According to a theory that is generally accepted today, the Moon was created as a result of a violent collision between young planet Earth and an asteroid the size of Mars. The impact hurled massive amounts of rock from Earth and from the shattered asteroid into space. Under Earth's force of attraction, the rock fragments began to circle around our planet, eventually joining together to form the Moon.

Destination: the Moon

On July 21, 1969, a human being stepped onto the surface of the Moon for the first time. The man was Neil Armstrong, member of the Apollo 11 mission. Following this memorable date, five other missions touched down on the Moon. In all, a dozen astronauts have visited our natural satellite. They have taken many photographs, conducted a variety of scientific experiments, and collected close to 880 pounds (400 kg) of lunar rocks. Americans are planning to return to the Moon in 2015. In preparation for this future mission, they will first send space probes to explore the surface. They plan to construct a permanent lunar base that will serve as a launching site for future flights to Mars and beyond. To this day, the Moon is the only celestial body that has been visited by humans.

In the lunar sky

Viewed from the Moon, Earth appears four times as large as the Moon does when it's viewed from our planet. Earth is also 60 times brighter. The lack of atmosphere on the Moon allows astronauts to observe our own beautiful blue-and-white planet with amazing clarity. Members of the Apollo missions have said that watching Earth rise in the Moon's dark sky was a spectacle of extraordinary beauty.

By the light of the silvery Moon

...g ago, people worshipped the Moon and believed it had magical powers. Some thought that the light of the full moon could turn people into werewolves. In spite of their fears, people used the light of the Moon to help them travel at night. Next to the Sun, the Moon is the brightest object in the sky. However, it does not produce light by itself the way the Sun does; instead it acts like a mirror, reflecting light from the Sun. Night after night, the Moon seems to change its shape in the sky, turning from a thin crescent into a full circle. While the Moon travels around Earth, the Sun lights the satellite's surface, either partially or fully. These different faces, which are called Moon phases, follow a cycle that lasts 29 $1/2$ days.

See activity p. 74

LUNAR ECLIPSES

Lunar eclipses have been observed since the beginning of time. The cause of these phenomena was first described by the Greek philosopher Thales about 2,600 years ago. A lunar eclipse occurs when Earth passes between the Moon and the Sun. The Moon falls entirely under Earth's shadow and is plunged into darkness. Lunar eclipses happen more often than eclipses of the Sun. Unlike solar eclipses, however, lunar eclipses can be observed safely with the naked eye.

Earth

Shadow zone

Eclipsed Moon

Sun

Even though the Moon's gravity is six times weaker than Earth's, its force of attraction is powerful enough to pull water from Earth's oceans up toward itself. The "bulge" or "swelling" that occurs in the ocean is called a high tide. At the same time, water is drawn away from the beaches on each side of the bulge, producing a low tide in those areas. The oceans that are facing away from the Moon also experience the same effects. That is why tides occur twice a day: as an ocean faces the Moon and as it faces away from the Moon. When the Sun and the Moon are aligned in a straight line with Earth, the tides reach their maximum height. These kinds of tides are called spring tides and occur when there is a new or a full moon.

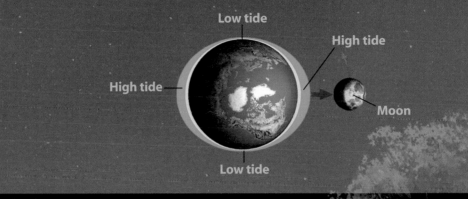

Low tide

High tide

High tide

Moon

Low tide

The man in the Moon

With a bit of imagination, it's possible to see a face when looking at the Moon with the naked eye. That is why people often say that there is a man in the Moon. The dark spots make up the eyes, the nose, and the mouth. These dark spots are, in fact, the Moon's huge, dusty plains. Early astronomers once thought these plains were seas, and so they named them Ocean of Storms, Sea of Tranquility, and Lake of Dreams. The rest of the man's face is formed by the Moon's hills and mountain ranges.

Rocks around the Sun

After the planets and their natural satellites, asteroids are the biggest objects in our solar system. They travel around the Sun on a path called an orbit, the same way the planets do. When the solar system was created, asteroids formed out of the leftover materials that did not go into making the Sun and the planets. Unlike the planets, which are round, asteroids are potato-shaped, and are made up of rocks, ice, and metals. They are also much smaller than the planets, measuring from a few inches (centimeters) to a few hundred miles (kilometers) long. In 1801, Italian astronomer Giuseppe Piazzi discovered the first asteroid and named it Ceres. Measuring more than 600 miles (1,000 km) across, Ceres was thought to be the largest asteroid until Quaoar was discovered in 2002. Measuring 1,000 miles (1,600 km) across, 2004 DW is now the largest known asteroid.

THE MAIN ASTEROID BELT

There are a few million asteroids located in the vast space between Mars and Jupiter, making up what is known as the Main asteroid belt.

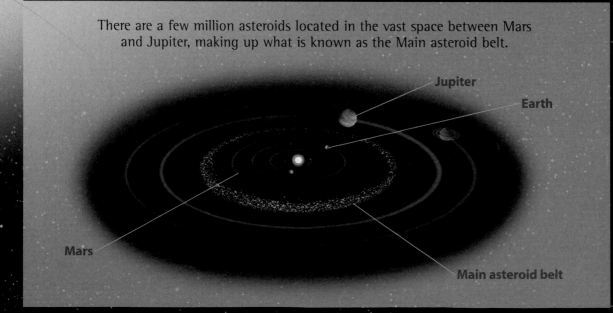

Jupiter

Earth

Mars

Main asteroid belt

Watching the asteroids

As they travel around the Sun, some asteroids can be spotted regularly heading on a course for Earth. Scientists are particularly interested in these so-called "Earth-crossers" because of the possibility that one of them may one day collide with our planet. Observation programs, like the American SpaceWatch, keep a close lookout for Earth-crossers. If one of these asteroids ever appears to be on a course for our planet, scientists hope to knock it off its path or destroy it before it reaches Earth. Space probes, like NEAR (Near Earth Asteroid Rendezvous), are also studying these asteroids. Since NEAR was first launched in 1996, it has managed to photograph amazing images of two asteroids: Mathilde, measuring 37 miles (60 km) long, and Eros, 20.5 miles (33 km) long.

Naming the asteroids

According to tradition, a new asteroid is always named by its discoverer. Among the 40,000 asteroids that have been officially named, we find characters from Greek myths, scientists, and famous artists. For instance, asteroids have been named after important painters like Picasso, storybook characters, such as Merlin the magician and Pinocchio, and novelists like Tolkien, author of *The Lord of the Rings* trilogy. Even popular singers like Elvis Presley have been honored with an asteroid, joining the ranks of great classical music composers like Bach and Beethoven.

Spectacular visitors

The people of ancient times were afraid of comets—strange balls of light that occasionally lit up the night sky and seemed to appear from out of nowhere. They were seen as a sign of bad things to come, bringing earthquakes, famines, illnesses, death, and destruction. A comet streaking across the sky is without a doubt an amazing spectacle, but it is actually nothing more than a huge, dirty snowball traveling through the solar system. Comets are visible to us only when they get close enough to the Sun. The Sun's heat vaporizes some of the ice they contain, causing the comet to release long trails of gases and dust particles that act like mirrors and reflect the solar rays. Some comets come back at regular intervals. These visitors are called periodic comets. Comet Hale-Bopp, for instance, was visible in our night skies for several weeks in the spring of 1997. It will return in about 2,400 years.

Gas tail

Dust tail

Coma
The coma is formed around the comet's small nucleus, at the center, by the heat of the Sun. It looks like thick hair around a small face (in fact, the word "comet" comes from the Greek *komêtês*, which means "long-haired"). The coma is mainly made up of water vapor and carbon dioxide.

Nucleus
The small nucleus, or center, is hidden by the coma. Every time a comet gets close to the Sun, the nucleus heats up and sheds some of the ice, gases, and rock particles that it is composed of. After about 500 trips around the Sun, all that is left of the comet is often just a chunk of rock that looks like an asteroid.

Where do comets come from?

Astronomers think that some comets originate in the Oort
cloud, a vast area In space, billions of miles (kilometers) beyond
Pluto's orbit. This distant formation surrounding the solar
system contains billions of chunks of dirty ice measuring about
6 miles (10 km) across. Other comets originate in the Kuiper
belt, an area extending beyond Neptune's orbit. This ring of
comets contains more than 35,000 frozen objects measuring
more than 63 miles (100 km) across. Now and again, a chunk of
frozen material leaves the Oort cloud or the Kuiper belt and
goes into orbit around the Sun. At least 900 such comets are
known to be traveling around our star.

Tail

Most of the time we can only make out a single long tail in the sky,
but comets actually have two tails. One is made of gas, and the
other is made of dust. This bright double tail is the most spectacular
part of the comet. Its shape may vary, depending on what the
comet is made of and the strength of solar wind, a gale of highly
excited particles that rush away from the Sun. The comet's tail never
points toward the Sun because solar winds propel the tail to the
rear. A comet's tail can stretch for millions of miles (kilometers).

Rocks from the sky

A shooting star is not a star at all. It is a meteor—a brief streak of light formed by a small rock that burns brightly as it enters Earth's atmosphere. There are billions of them floating around in space. They are pieces of asteroids and dust from comets. As they travel at more than 62,000 miles per hour (100,000 km/h), friction from the air heats them up and sets them on fire. Sometimes, big rocks crash to Earth without entirely burning up. These are called meteorites. The largest of the 3,000 meteorites found so far fell in Namibia, Africa, thousands of years ago. It is 8 feet (2.5 m) long and weighs 60 tons (55 metric tons)—about the weight of 10 elephants! All meteorites are studied and carefully preserved in museums and universities. Along with the Moon rocks brought back by astronauts, they are the only extraterrestrial materials scientists have to study.

The end of the dinosaurs
Dinosaurs vanished from Earth 65 million years ago. Some scientists believe that their mysterious disappearance was partly caused by the impact of a meteorite that fell near the Yucatán Peninsula in Mexico. This giant rock would have begun to burn as it fell through the atmosphere, starting enormous fires on Earth after it landed. Smoke and clouds of ash would have covered the skies over more than half of the planet. As large areas of Earth were plunged into darkness, plants would have died from lack of sunlight to help them grow. Without plants to eat, many animals, including the dinosaurs, would have died of hunger.

The best-preserved crater

The famous Meteor Crater was created by the impact of a meteorite that fell in the Arizona desert 50,000 years ago. By studying this scar on the land, which measures three-quarters of a mile (1.2 km) across and 570 feet (175 m) deep, scientists have calculated that an enormous meteorite weighing no less than 110,000 tons (100,000 metric tons) was responsible. Scientists believe the Meteor Crater, also known as the Barringer Meteorite Crater, is the most recently formed crater on Earth. It is also one of the best preserved because so little rain has fallen on the area to wear the crater down.

Earth is growing!

Every year, at least 44,000 tons (40,000 metric tons) of tiny meteorites fall to Earth. Because these bits of dust are too light to reach high speeds, they do not burn up as they enter our atmosphere. Earth is growing by more than 110 tons (100 metric tons) a day thanks to these materials that it sweeps up as it travels through space!

Space exploration

Over the years, astronomers have developed increasingly sophisticated instruments for observing, analyzing, and understanding the phenomena that take place in the universe. Astronauts on spaceships have left Earth to explore the Moon or do other work in space. Probes have been sent out to explore the planets that are too distant or unsafe for humans to visit. The exploration of the universe continues to be an adventure full of surprises, twists, and turns.

Looking farther into space

For more than 5,000 years, astronomers observed the skies using only their eyes. They were able to identify five planets, dozens of constellations, and thousands of stars. With the invention of the telescope in the late 1500s, however, new enlarged views of the skies transformed the science of astronomy. Today's powerful telescopes allow us to observe celestial objects that are very far away. Celestial objects give off visible light as well as different kinds of rays, such as X rays or radio waves. A new generation of telescopes is able to capture these invisible rays. Ground-based radio telescopes using gigantic antennas, for instance, can tune into radio waves emitted by stars or by distant galaxies. Other kinds of equipment, such as satellite observatories, are put into orbit more than 315 miles (500 km) above Earth to look for the kinds of rays that are blocked by our planet's atmosphere. Earth-based astronomers can watch the images on-screen. In fact, today's astronomers spend more time studying the images recorded in their computers than looking at the skies.

The biggest of them all
The most powerful telescopes are usually inside observatories on mountaintops where visibility is greatest. On Mount Mauna Kea, in Hawaii, there are several international telescopes, two of which are the twin Keck telescopes. Sitting at an altitude of 2.6 miles (4.1 km) high, the Keck telescopes are the largest and most powerful in the world. Their primary mirrors measure 32 feet (10 m) across—that's longer than six bicycles laid end to end! Each giant mirror is actually made up of 36 individual mirrors. The twin telescopes are able to operate together or separately.

Reflecting telescopes produce enlarged images of distant celestial objects using two mirrors. The first one, called the primary mirror, sits at the bottom of the telescope tube and acts the way a lens would. It catches the light given off by distant objects, and then sends it to the secondary mirror. This secondary mirror guides the light rays to the eyepiece through which the astronomer can view the image. The larger the primary mirror, the more powerful the telescope, and the farther into space it can look. Some mirrors measure several yards (meters) across, while others are made up of several smaller mirrors placed side by side. A computer adjusts the individual mirrors so they are set in such a way that they function as one large mirror.

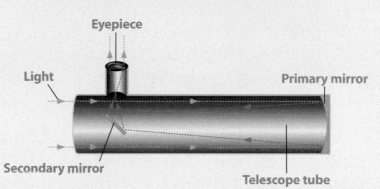

Eyepiece

Light

Primary mirror

Secondary mirror

Telescope tube

Fuzzy images

In 1990, the Hubble Space Telescope was put into orbit around Earth. Soon after its launch, the powerful instrument began sending fuzzy pictures. As it turned out, the primary mirror was not working properly. In 1993, a team of astronauts from the space shuttle Endeavour installed "eyeglasses" on the Hubble's mirror. Since the corrective device was added to the mirror, the telescope has been sending back some of the most extraordinary images ever seen from space.

The conquest of space

In 1961, Soviet cosmonaut Yuri Gagarin became the first human to venture into space. Eight years later, American astronaut Neil Armstrong walked on the Moon. These two memorable events marked the beginning of the conquest of space. They became possible thanks to the invention of the rocket. Besides allowing people to travel above Earth, a rocket's job is to put a payload—a space probe or an artificial satellite—into space. Space probes are like remote-controlled robots, and are sent into space to study objects that are too distant or not suitable for people to visit. Artificial satellites are also put into orbit around Earth. Some of them are used in telecommunications and can transmit television broadcasts around the world. Other satellites are used to study the Sun or to help meteorologists forecast tornadoes.

Modern-day explorers

Space probes have been exploring our solar system since 1959. They have visited every planet except Pluto. Some probes travel from one planet to the next, while others go into orbit around a particular planet and remain there. These modern-day explorers take photographs, analyze samples, and take many different kinds of measurements. The data that is collected is transmitted by radio signal back to scientists on Earth. Once the mission is over, the unmanned space probe doesn't usually return to Earth. Instead it either leaves our solar system and continues on toward the stars, or it falls onto the Sun and burns.

A pool of fuel!

At takeoff, a rocket burns more than 595,000 gallons (2,250,000 l) of fuel in just three seconds—enough fuel to fill an Olympic-size swimming pool!

ROCKETS IN SPACE

To escape Earth's force of attraction, an object would have to reach a speed of 25,000 miles per hour (40,000 km/h). Rockets are one of the rare vehicles designed to achieve this high speed. By burning fuel in record time, a rocket engine produces huge quantities of hot gases. The gases are forced through its nozzles below, propelling the rocket upward in the opposite direction. Rocket fuel needs oxygen to burn, and because there is no oxygen in space, rockets need to carry their own supply. Most rockets are constructed in several detachable sections called stages. Each stage contains its own engines, fuel, and oxygen tanks. Each section can be dropped as it runs out of fuel, and the next stage takes over. This helps the rocket become lighter and move more easily.

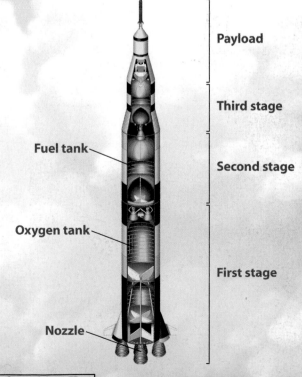

Payload

Third stage

Fuel tank

Second stage

Oxygen tank

First stage

Nozzle

See activity p. 75

Humans in space

Since the first astronaut explored space in 1961, more than 400 men and women have taken part in space missions. Astronauts today mainly travel onboard space shuttles. Unlike rockets, which can only be used once, shuttles can make many trips—to repair a damaged satellite, for example, or to visit a space station. A space station is a laboratory orbiting around Earth, where astronauts live and work for several months at a time. Right now, at least 16 countries are working together on a highly complex laboratory called the International Space Station. Expected to be operating by the year 2006, its opening date was postponed because of the explosion onboard the Columbia space shuttle in February 2003. Columbia was one of the shuttles transporting building materials for the space station. The purpose of future flights will be to assemble the International Space Station. The United States plans to return to the Moon in 2015. They expect to establish a permanent base there, from which they can one day launch flights to Mars and beyond.

The life of an astronaut

The conditions onboard a spaceship are not like those on an airplane. No longer affected by Earth's gravity, astronauts and any loose objects on the shuttle float about weightlessly. Weightlessness turns the most ordinary task into a major challenge. Astronauts often need to anchor themselves with straps. Besides changing their way of eating, sleeping, or going to the bathroom, weightlessness changes blood circulation and weakens muscles. Astronauts must be careful to eat well and to exercise in order to stay healthy. When they leave the vessel to do repairs, for example, astronauts put on space suits. Besides supplying them with oxygen to breathe, the suits protect against the cold as well as the harmful rays of the Sun.

THE SPACE SHUTTLE

During the 1960s and 1970s, American astronauts returned to Earth in capsules that landed in the ocean. With the construction of the first space shuttle in 1981, returning astronauts no longer had to be fished out of the ocean because the shuttle could land them comfortably like an airplane. At launch time, the main section called the orbiter sits on top of a huge tank containing fuel for the engines. Behind the compartment that houses the team of five to seven astronauts is a cargo load, which may contain a satellite or even a space probe, depending on the mission.

1. Launch
At launch, two booster rockets and the liquid-fuel engines fire up together, generating enough thrust for liftoff.

2. The booster rockets are dropped.
Two minutes after launch, the empty booster rockets parachute into the ocean, where they are recovered. Once they are overhauled, the booster rockets are put back into service on other missions.

3. The fuel tank is dropped.
After eight minutes of flight, the huge, empty exterior fuel tank is dropped. As it falls through the atmosphere, it burns up and the ashes are strewn over the ocean.

4. In orbit
Ten minutes after launch, the shuttle is in orbit. It now circles around the Earth at a speed of 17,000 miles per hour (28,000 km/h) for one or two weeks, depending on the mission.

5. Reentry
To return to Earth, the pilot slows down the speed of the shuttle. As it loses speed, Earth's gravity pulls it down. This alters the shuttle's orbit, and it begins to descend through Earth's atmosphere at a very high speed, while heating up from the friction with the air. More than 30,000 ceramic tiles on the shuttle's exterior surface protect it against the intense heat.

6. Landing
With its engines shut down, the shuttle glides in for a smooth landing on the runway, just like an airplane.

Are we alone?

Earth seems to be the only planet that supports life. But because there are probably billions of other solar systems similar to ours, some scientists think that there may be another planet with conditions that promote life. Since the early 1960s, a number of astronomers have been searching for extraterrestrial civilizations. By pointing gigantic radio telescopes toward distant stars, they hope to capture signals from other intelligent beings. For a few years now, a new science called astrobiology has tried to determine what conditions are necessary to maintain life. Ever since tiny living organisms were discovered in hostile environments like the dry, frozen valleys of Antarctica, researchers have been convinced that life could develop in extremely difficult conditions elsewhere in the universe. Only time will tell if life is so rare that it only exists on planet Earth.

Interstellar messages

Astronomers regularly send messages into space that are intended for possible extraterrestrials, inhabitants of other planets. These messages are sent in the form of radio waves, or engraved on disks and plates and then put onboard space probes. The Pioneer probes, which are on their way to the stars, are carrying an image representing a man and a woman as well as our position in the solar system. The Voyager 1 and 2 probes are carrying a gold disk with sound and images representative of Earth, including birdsongs and greetings in 55 languages. Considering the speed at which these messengers are traveling, they're due to arrive at their destinations in a few hundred thousand years!

I saw a BIFO!

Even if many people are convinced they've seen a flying saucer, no space vessel piloted by extraterrestrials has ever been officially observed. Most of the strange lights or oddly shaped objects that people see are nothing more than planets, satellites, comets, or meteors. One could say that these UFOs are actually BIFOs, not Unidentified Flying Objects, but Badly Identified Flying Objects!

The conditions necessary for life

Since Earth is neither too close nor too far from the Sun, it is able to maintain an average surface temperature of 57°F (14°C). Earth can only sustain this temperature because of the atmosphere that blankets it. Gases in the atmosphere trap the Sun's heat and allow water to exist in liquid form, which is essential to life as we know it. Clouds in the atmosphere distribute water over the surface of the planet in the form of rain or snow. Earth's atmosphere also helps to shield us from meteorites, solar wind, and some of the Sun's harmful rays. It is the combination of all of these factors that has permitted life to thrive on Earth in so many different forms.

Facts

A guide to the main features of the nine planets in the solar system

	Mercury	Venus	Earth	Mars	Jupiter	Saturn	Uranus	Neptune	Pluto
Diameter in miles (km)	3,031 (4,878)	7,519 (12,100)	7,926 (12,756)	4,217 (6,787)	88,846 (142,984)	74,898 (120,536)	31,757 (51,108)	30,781 (49,538)	1,460 (2,350)
Distance from the Sun in millions of miles (millions km)	36 (58)	67 (108)	93 (150)	142 (228)	483 (778)	888 (1,429)	1,786 (2,875)	2,799 (4,504)	3,675 (5,915)
Average temperatures in °F (°C)	-292 to 800 (-180 to 427)	887 (475)	68 (20)	-189 to 70 (-123 to 20)	-166 (-110)	-292 (-180)	-364 (-220)	-382 (-230)	-396 (-238)
Duration of a day	58.6 days	243 days	23.9 hours	24.6 hours	9.8 hours	10.6 hours	17.2 hours	16.1 hours	6.3 days
Duration of a year	87.9 days	224.7 days	365.25 days	687 days	11.8 years	29.4 years	83.7 years	163.7 years	248.5 years
Number of known moons	0	0	1	2	63	31	27	13	1
Number of known rings	0	0	0	0	3	thousands	11	4	0
Visits by space probes	1	22	0	16	6	4	1	1	0

Note: If you want to remember the order of the planets in the solar system, keep this handy phrase in mind: My Very Easy Map Just Shows Us Nine Planets.

The 10 brightest stars

Viewed from Earth, the stars do not all seem to shine with the same intensity. A star may appear less bright than another because it is farther away or because it produces less light. Rigel and Betelgeuse, for example, seem almost equally bright, but Rigel is almost twice as far away from Earth and about four times brighter than Betelgeuse. The apparent magnitude of a star—how bright it appears in the sky—can be measured on a scale. The brighter the star is, the lower the number of its apparent magnitude. Very brilliant stars have magnitudes of zero or even negative numbers.

Name	Constellation	Color	Apparent magnitude	Distance from Earth (in light-years)
Sirius	Greater Dog	White	- 1.46	8.6
Canopus	Keel	White	- 0.72	313
Arcturus	Herdsman	Orange	- 0.04	36.7
Alpha Centauri	Centaur	Yellow	- 0.00	4.3
Vega	Lyre	White	+ 0.03	25.3
Capella	Charioteer	Yellow	+ 0.08	42
Rigel	Orion	Blue-white	+ 0.12	773
Procyon	Lesser Dog	White	+ 0.38	11.4
Achernar	Eridanus	Blue-white	+ 0.46	144
Betelgeuse	Orion	Red	+ 0.50	522

Total eclipses of the Sun between now and 2015

Solar eclipses always occur during the daytime, in an area limited to a few hundred square miles (square kilometers). Total eclipses of the Sun last a maximum of seven minutes. You must never look directly at the Sun—not with your naked eye and especially not with binoculars or a telescope, even if the Sun is hidden during an eclipse. This can seriously damage your eyes!

Date	Ideal observation site
April 8, 2005	Eastern Pacific, Central America
March 29, 2006	Northern Africa, central Asia, Atlantic
August 1, 2008	Northern Canada, Greenland, Siberia, China
July 22, 2009	India, Nepal, China, central Pacific
July 11, 2010	South Pacific, Chile, Argentina
November 13, 2012	Northern Australia, South Pacific
November 3, 2013	Atlantic, central Africa
March 20, 2015	Northeastern Atlantic

Total eclipses of the Moon between now and 2015

Lunar eclipses, unlike solar eclipses, can be safely observed with the naked eye. Lunar eclipses are less spectacular, but they occur more frequently and last longer (about one hour).

Date	Ideal observation site
March 3, 2007	Africa, Europe
August 28, 2007	Central Pacific, western America
February 21, 2008	North America, South America, western Europe
December 21, 2010	North America, western South America
June 15, 2011	Southwest Asia, Africa, Indian Ocean
December 10, 2011	Western Pacific, eastern Asia, Alaska, Yukon
April 15, 2014	Western North and South America, Pacific
October 8, 2014	Pacific, western North and South America
April 4, 2015	Pacific, western North and South America
September 28, 2015	Western Africa, western Europe, North America, South America

Famous meteor showers

Earth frequently crosses the path of an old comet. When the rock particles and dust left behind by the comet enter Earth's atmosphere, they burn up and produce a meteor shower. Some famous meteor showers can be observed at specific times of the year. Meteor showers seem to come from very precise areas in the sky, within the boundaries of one or two constellations.

Name of meteor shower	Constellations to watch	Dates (maximum)	Number of meteors per hour	Related object
Quadrantid	Herdsman	January 3–4	8–40	unknown
Lyrid	Hercules-Lyre	April 21–22	8	Thatcher's Comet
Eta Aquarid	Aquarius-Pisces	May 4–5	6	Halley's Comet
Delta Aquarid	Aquarius	July 28–29	20	unknown
Perseid	Perseus	August 12–13	70	Swift-Tuttle Comet
Orionid	Orion	October 21–22	20	Halley's Comet
Taurid	Taurus	November 2–3	15	Encke's Comet
Leonid	Leo	November 17–18	20	Tempel-Tuttle Comet
Geminid	Gemini	December 13–14	18–50	3200 Phaeton
Ursid	Lesser Bear	December 22–23	20	Tuttle's Comet

The sky of the Northern Hemisphere

We can draw figures in the sky by tracing lines between the bright points of the stars. These figures are called constellations. More than 2,000 years ago, the ancient Greeks and Romans identified about two-thirds of the 88 constellations we know today. It often takes a lot of imagination, however, to recognize the people, animals, or objects they are supposed to represent! The constellations that are visible in the sky of the Northern Hemisphere are not the same as those we see in the sky of the Southern Hemisphere. In both hemispheres, different constellations come into view as Earth makes its journey around the Sun. For this reason there are different maps of the sky for each hemisphere and for different times of the year. The map illustrated here shows the main constellations that can be seen in the Northern Hemisphere every night of the year at 10 P.M. (or one hour later in summer if clocks are set to daylight saving time).

Leo

Leo is one of the oldest known constellations. The Sumerians (the first inhabitants of Mesopotamia—present-day Iraq) identified it more than 6,000 years ago. Throughout history and across cultures, people have recognized the lion's head shape that is formed by the stars on the right of the constellation.

Great Bear

Great Bear is without doubt the most well known constellation. It is easily recognizable by the seven bright stars that form the tail and part of the back of the bear. The Big Dipper, which is often mistaken for a constellation, actually belongs to this group of stars and forms the saucepan shape we see below the bear's back. The other stars that make up Great Bear are less bright, and can be spotted more easily on a very dark night.

The Northern sky

The globe of the Earth is divided into two halves, or hemispheres, by the equator. The Northern sky covers the upper half of the globe. Its constellations are visible from the Northern Hemisphere, which includes Europe, the United States, Canada, and Japan.

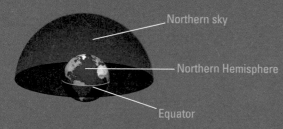

Northern sky

Northern Hemisphere

Equator

Taurus

Pictures of Taurus have been found on clay tablets dating back to the golden age of Mesopotamia, more than 3,000 years ago.

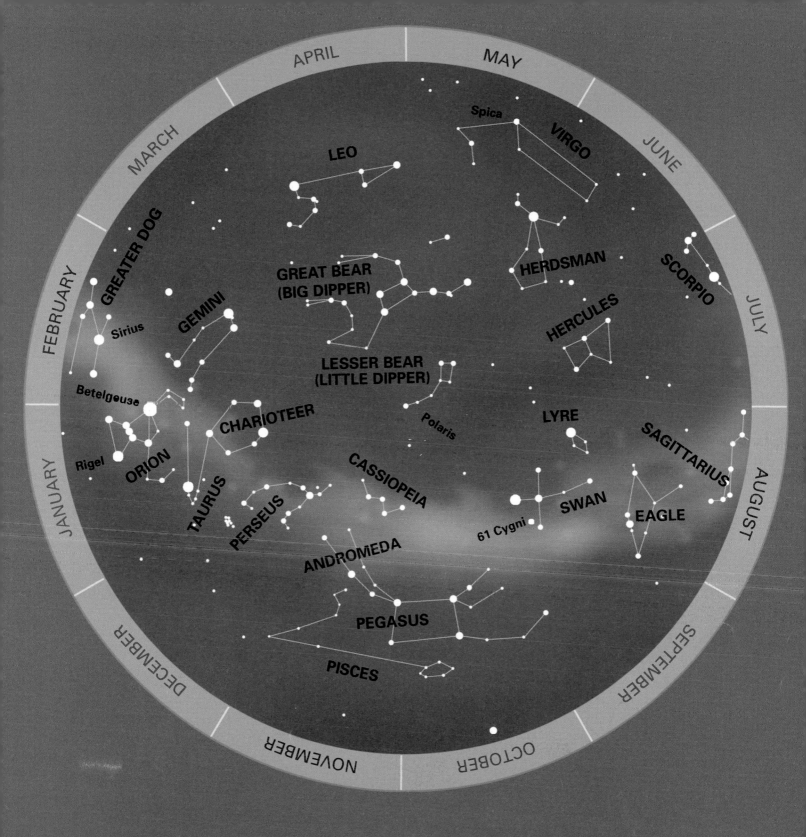

How to use this chart

After choosing the map of the sky for the hemisphere where you live, place this book on a flat surface. With the help of a compass, find North, if you are using the chart of the Northern Hemisphere, or South, if you are using the chart for the Southern Hemisphere. Turn the chart until the top of the page is pointing in that direction. Now rotate the chart until the current month appears at the top. The stars shown in the center of the chart can be found in the sky directly overhead, and the stars shown at the edges of the chart can be seen along the horizon. Once the chart is placed in the proper position, look for a very bright star or an easily recognizable shape.

The sky of the Southern Hemisphere

While most of the constellations in the Northern sky were named by the ancient Greeks and Romans more than 2,000 years ago, the constellations of the Southern Hemisphere were identified much later. They were not visible to the ancient Mediterranean astronomers, so they were not named until European explorers ventured south of the equator in the 17th and 18th centuries. This chart shows the Southern sky's main constellations. They are visible all year round at 10 P.M. (or one hour later in summer if clocks are set to daylight saving time). The Southern sky is visible in major regions of the Southern Hemisphere, which include South America, South Africa, Australia, and New Zealand.

The Southern sky

The Southern sky covers the lower half of our globe. Its constellations are visible from the Southern Hemisphere. The oval line shows the path of the Sun in the sky, called the ecliptic.

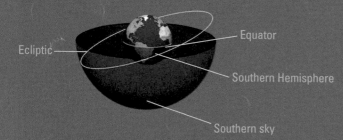

Ecliptic

Equator

Southern Hemisphere

Southern sky

The zodiac and astrology

The zodiac is a narrow area of the sky along which the Sun, the Moon, and the planets seem to move. While traveling this celestial route during the course of a year, the Sun crosses the path of the 12 constellations in the zodiac—Pisces, Aries, Taurus, Gemini, Cancer, Leo, Virgo, Libra, Scorpio, Sagittarius, Capricorn, and Aquarius. Astrologers believe that the position of the stars and the planets on the day of one's birth determines a person's personality. A person's astrological sign corresponds to the constellation nearest the Sun at the time of one's birth. Astrological dates today, however, no longer match true astronomical dates. For example, the month of the zodiac sign Virgo runs from August 23 to September 22. In reality, however, the Sun moves through Virgo between September 17 and October 31. Because science has never been able to demonstrate that the stars influence a person's personality, most scientists think that astrology is pure superstition.

The Southern Cross

The Southern Cross is the most famous of the Southern sky constellations. It is one of the smallest constellations, and its main stars are among the brightest in the sky. Before the Southern Cross was identified in 1515, its stars were considered part of the Centaur constellation.

Orion

Orion is one of the most spectacular constellations in the sky. It is clearly visible above the horizon. Its outline represents the hunter Orion, the son of the god of the sea in Greek and Roman mythology. Two bright stars—the large red star Betelgeuse and the large blue star Rigel—form the shoulder and the foot of the hunter. Orion is easy to spot because three of its stars line up to form the hunter's belt. This constellation, visible in the skies of both hemispheres, is a handy reference point for locating other constellations.

Virgo

Virgo is a large constellation. According to mythology, Virgo represents the goddess of the harvest and carries a bundle of wheat.

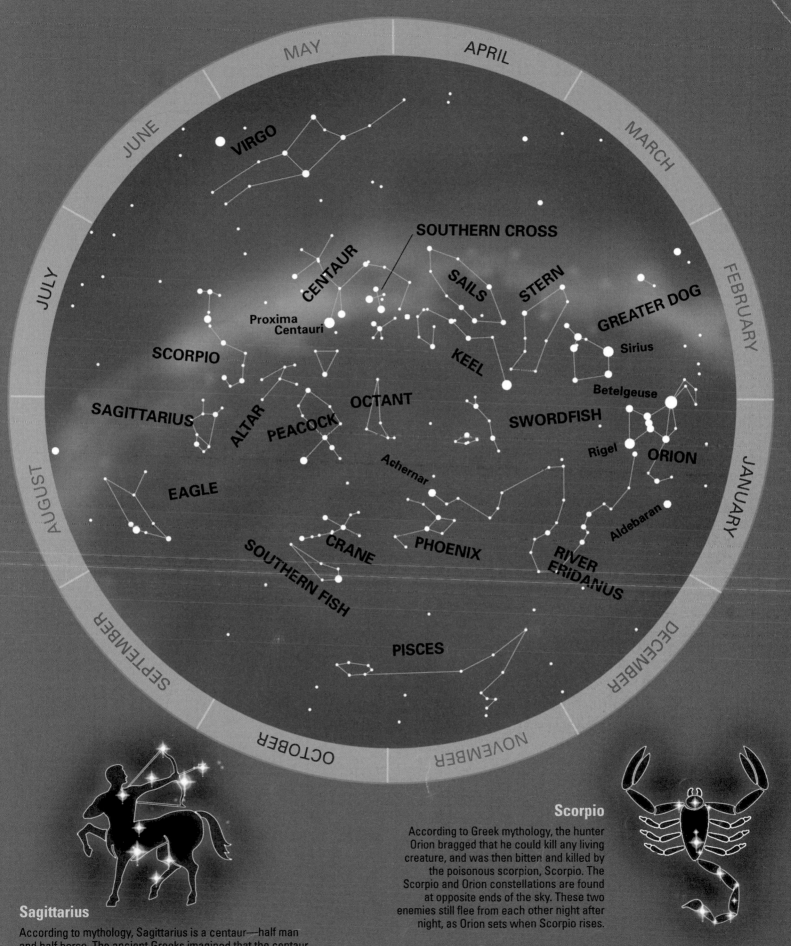

MAY
APRIL
JUNE
MARCH
JULY
FEBRUARY
AUGUST
JANUARY
SEPTEMBER
DECEMBER
OCTOBER
NOVEMBER

VIRGO

SOUTHERN CROSS

CENTAUR

SAILS

STERN

GREATER DOG

Proxima
Centauri

Sirius

KEEL

SCORPIO

Betelgeuse

SAGITTARIUS

OCTANT

SWORDFISH

ALTAR

PEACOCK

Rigel

ORION

EAGLE

Achernar

Aldebaran

CRANE

PHOENIX

SOUTHERN FISH

RIVER
ERIDANUS

PISCES

Sagittarius

According to mythology, Sagittarius is a centaur—half man
and half horse. The ancient Greeks imagined that the centaur
was armed with a bow, ready to shoot an arrow.

Scorpio

According to Greek mythology, the hunter
Orion bragged that he could kill any living
creature, and was then bitten and killed by
the poisonous scorpion, Scorpio. The
Scorpio and Orion constellations are found
at opposite ends of the sky. These two
enemies still flee from each other night after
night, as Orion sets when Scorpio rises.

Activities

Recreate the phases of the Moon

You've noticed that the Moon doesn't always have the same shape in the sky. Perform the following experiment and you'll understand why.

Necessary materials

To perform your experiment, you'll have to go into a dark room with no sunlight. Ideally, you should be able to turn out the lights in the room. The darker it is, the easier it will be to observe the phases of the Moon.

• A flashlight   • An inflated balloon   • A sheet of aluminum foil big enough to cover the balloon entirely

Experiment

1. Wrap the aluminum foil around the entire balloon.

2. Set the flashlight on a piece of furniture so that its beam shines above the top of your head. Turn off the lights and stand in front of the flashlight.

3. Hold the balloon at arm's length so that it's lit by the flashlight, then slowly turn your body around in a circle. Don't take your eyes off the balloon. Notice the way that it's lit.

Observe carefully

In this experiment, the balloon plays the role of the Moon, while the flashlight replaces the Sun—and you represent the Earth.

When the balloon is lined up perfectly between you and the flashlight, its visible face looks black. In space, this is the moment when the Moon has its "back" lit by the Sun. Seen from Earth, its face, or front, is dark: that is the new Moon.

In contrast, when your body is between the flashlight and the balloon, the visible face of the balloon is fully lit. In space, this is the moment when the front of the Moon is lit by the Sun. Seen from Earth, its face is completely luminous: that is the full Moon.

The different zones of shadow and light that you observe on the balloon between these two moments correspond to the different phases of the Moon!

Recreate the solar system step by step

The distances between planets in the solar system are so great they're hard to imagine. Create your own solar system! It will help you imagine those distances.

Necessary materials

It is best to conduct this experiment outside on the sidewalk.

• Big sticks of chalk   • 11 stones (1 very big, 4 big, 2 medium, 2 small, and 2 small pebbles)

Experiment

1. Start your solar system by placing the biggest stone at your feet. Next to it, write SUN.

2. Rest your heel against the big stone. Halfway along your foot place a small stone. Next to it, write MERCURY.

3. At the joint in your big toe, place a medium stone. Next to it, write VENUS.

4. At the tip of your toe place the other medium stone. Next to it, write EARTH. And just next to it, place a small pebble—this is the Moon.

5. Now step forward, placing the heel of one foot just ahead of the toes of the other, and count one and a half feet from the Sun. Place your last small stone. Next to it, write MARS. For a better effect, place all the stones in a straight line.

6. Five feet from the Sun, place a big stone. Next to it, write JUPITER.

7. Nine and a half feet from the Sun, place a big stone. Next to it, write SATURN.

8. Nineteen feet from the Sun, place a big stone. Next to it, write URANUS.

9. Thirty feet from the Sun, place the last big stone. Next to it, write NEPTUNE.

10. Finally, 40 feet from the Sun, place your last small pebble. Next to it, write PLUTO.

Observe carefully

The planets closest to the Sun, the internal planets, are closer to one another than the giant, or gaseous, planets, while Pluto is off by itself.

Make a rocket take off

Isn't it incredible that heavy rockets can take off from the ground and be propelled into space? In this experiment you will build your own rocket—and have fun making it take off!

Necessary materials

It is best to conduct this experiment outside because the mixture of water and acid indigestion tablets can make a mess.

- A ruler

- A pencil

- A small plastic container with a lid (a film container would be perfect)

- A sheet of paper 8 1/2 in. (21 1/2 cm) wide by 11 in. (28 cm) long

- Tape

- Scissors

- Water

- Effervescent tablets, like Alka-Seltzer, for acid indigestion (these can be found in any drugstore—ask an adult to help you find them)

- Safety goggles

Experiment

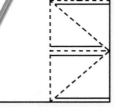

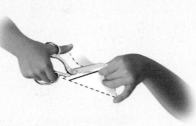

1. On the sheet of paper, copy the dotted lines and the solid lines as they appear in the drawing above.

2. Cut along the dotted lines as shown in the drawing.

3. Fold along the solid lines as shown in the drawing.

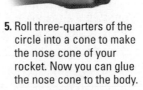

4. Tape the small plastic container, open end down, onto the lower edge of the paper rectangle, then roll it up to form the body of your rocket.

5. Roll three-quarters of the circle into a cone to make the nose cone of your rocket. Now you can glue the nose cone to the body.

6. Glue the wings to the body of the rocket.

7. Turn the rocket over and fill the small plastic container one-third full of water.

8. Drop an effervescent tablet into the water and close the cover. Move quickly!

9. Place the "rocket" and its cover on a flat surface. Then step back and wait a few seconds.

Observe carefully

When the effervescent tablet lands in the water it dissolves and its thousands of little gas bubbles create pressure inside the plastic container. That pressure will become so strong, it will blow off the cover!

The rockets we send into space require a huge amount of fuel. When fuel burns, it produces hot gases that are violently expelled by the jets. This expulsion of gas is so powerful it creates a thrust that sends the rocket into orbit.

Glossary

A

astronaut
A person who travels in space on a spaceship. The Russians use the word *cosmonaut* while the French prefer *spationaute*.

astronomer
A scientist who studies celestial objects and the structure of the universe.

atmosphere
The layer of gas surrounding the surface of a planet, a natural satellite, or a star.

atom
The basic ingredient of matter. An atom is made up of a nucleus (which is made of protons and neutrons) around which one or several electrons travel.

axis
The imaginary line that runs through an object from top to bottom and around which the object rotates.

B

Big Bang
An event that may have occurred about 15 billion years ago that gave birth to all the matter in the universe. To this day, the Big Bang is the most widely accepted theory about how the universe was formed.

C

celestial body (celestial object)
A planet, a star, or any other natural object found in space.

chemical element
A substance that contains only one kind of atom.

crater
A hole created by the impact of a meteorite on the surface of a planet, a natural satellite, or an asteroid.

D

day
The time it takes for a planet to make a complete rotation around its own axis.

density
The mass of an object per unit of volume.

diameter
The length of a straight line that passes through the center of a round object.

E

electron
An elementary particle with a negative charge that orbits the nucleus of an atom.

elementary particle
A component of an atom that cannot be broken down into smaller particles.

ellipse
The oval-shaped path taken by orbiting celestial objects.

energy
The capacity of an object to perform work. There are different kinds of energy, such as heat, light, and electricity.

equator
An imaginary line that circles Earth midway between the two poles. It divides the planet into the Northern Hemisphere and the Southern Hemisphere.

extraterrestrial
Everything that comes from outside planet Earth. An inhabitant of another planet.

G

gas
A substance that is found naturally in a gaseous state. In a gas, the atoms are not attached to one another and take up all the available space.

gravity (gravitation)
The force of attraction between two bodies. In space, gravity creates the movement of the planets, the stars, and the galaxies. On Earth, it pulls objects toward the ground. The more compact and more massive the object, the larger its gravitational force.

H

helium
A simple chemical element. It is a very light gas found in great quantities in the stars (including the Sun).

hydrogen
The lightest gas and most abundant chemical element in the universe.

I

interstellar
Between the stars.

L

light-year
The distance that light travels in one year, moving at the speed of 186,000 miles per second (300,000 km/s), which is approximately 5,880 billion miles (9,460 billion km). A light-year is a unit of measurement for distance used by astronomers.

M

magnetic field
The area surrounding a body that exerts a magnetic force.

magnitude
The measurement of the brightness of a celestial body, particularly a star. The smaller the number, the brighter the body.

mass
The quantity of matter contained in an object.

matter
The substance that makes up an object.

methane
A gas that becomes explosive when combined with air. Methane can be produced by rotting plants, among other things.

mythology
A collection of myths and legends of a people. Many of the gods and heroes of Greek and Roman mythology have lent their names to celestial objects.

N

NASA
An American space agency (National Aeronautics and Space Administration).

neutron
An uncharged particle found in the nucleus of an atom.

nuclear fusion
A reaction during which the nuclei of atoms combine to form larger nuclei, resulting in the release of an enormous amount of energy.

nucleus
The central part of an atom, a comet, a galaxy, or a cell.

O

orbit
The path of a celestial object as it circles a planet or a star.

P

proton
A particle with a positive charge that, along with the neutron, makes up an atom's nucleus.

Q

quark
A charged elementary particle; a component of protons and neutrons.

S

satellite
A body that orbits in space around a larger celestial object. Moons are natural satellites that gravitate around planets. Artificial satellites are devices that are put into orbit around a celestial body, particularly Earth, by a rocket or a space shuttle.

space
The airless region beyond Earth's atmosphere.

subatomic particle
A component of an atom.

U

universe
Everything that exists. All the celestial objects found in space.

W

weight
The gravitational force exerted on an object; it varies according to the mass of the object.

weightlessness
The state of all living things and objects in the absence of Earth's force of attraction. Without apparent weight, they float freely in space.

Y

year
The time it takes for a planet to make a complete trip around the Sun.

Index

Bold = Main entry

Photo credits

Page 11, spiral galaxy: © NASA

Page 11, elliptical galaxy: © Anglo-Australian Observatory

Page 11, irregular galaxy: © NOAO/AURA/NSF/WIYN

Page 28, Mercury: © NSSDC/NASA

Page 30, Maat Mons: © JPL/CALTECH/NASA

Page 32, Earth landscape: © Corel Stock Photo Library

Page 36, Mars: © NSSDC/GSFC/NASA

Page 37, Martian landscape: © NASA/JPL/Cornell

Page 42, Miranda: © NSSDC/GSFC/NASA

Page 43, William Herschel: © Hulton-Deutsch
 Collection/CORBIS/Magmaphoto

Page 44, Triton: © JPL/NASA

Page 45, Johann Galle: © Astrophysikalisches Institut Postdam

Page 47, Clyde Tombaugh: © Lowell Observatory Archives

Page 53, NEAR: © JPL/NASA

Page 57, Meteor Crater: © D. Roddy/Lunar and Planetary Institute/IVV/NASA

Page 62, Mars Express: © JPL/NASA

Page 64, astronauts: © NASA

Page 67, tropical forest: © CORBIS/Magmaphoto

Jacket Photo Credits

star background: © Stock Trek/Photodisc/Picture Quest

top left: © Digital Vision/Picture Quest

top right: © Mike Brinson/The Image Bank/Getty Images

bottom middle: © James Porto/Taxi/Getty Images

Measurements

Most measurements in this book are written in abbreviated (shortened) form. Below you will find a key that explains what these abbreviations mean.

Key to abbreviations		
cm	=	centimeter
m	=	meter
km	=	kilometer
km/h	=	kilometers per hour
km/s	=	kilometers per second
in.	=	inch
ft	=	feet
mph	=	miles per hour
lb	=	pound

Conversion chart	
Metric	**U.S.**
1 cm	0.4 in.
1 m	3.28 ft
1 km	0.62 mile
10 km	6.21 miles
100 km	62.14 miles
1 kg	2.2 lbs
1 l	0.26 gallon